PROFILE OF THE A4s

Frontispiece: Illuminated by shafts of sunlight inside Newcastle Central in May 1938 is No. 4483 *Kingfisher* standing on the 'down' 'Flying Scotsman'.

W. B. Greenfield, NELPG Collection

Two pictures of *Golden Fleece* separated by almost twenty five years. *Above:*   In striking LNER Garter blue livery it is seen climbing away from Grantham, heading an express for King's Cross in 1938.

T. G. Hepburn, Rail Archive Stephenson

Below: On 4th October 1962, it is seen as BR No. 60030 shortly after leaving Leeds Central with the 12.55 express to King's Cross.
Gavin Morrison

Profile
of the
A4s

J. S. Whiteley and
G. W. Morrison

Oxford Publishing Company

INTRODUCTION

In 1935, the Silver Jubilee year of King George V, the first of the A4 streamlined Pacifics, designed by Nigel Gresley, appeared for service on the high-speed 'Silver Jubilee' express. The visual impact made by the appearance of this all streamlined train in its striking silver-grey livery has never been surpassed, and it is still hard to believe that actual construction of the first A4 took barely 12 weeks. Less than 3 weeks after delivery, and only three days before the 'Silver Jubilee' went into regular service *Silver Link* made its never to be forgotten trial publicity run with the new 'Silver Jubilee' stock, when a speed of 112½ m.p.h. was attained. Surely a sign of things to come, and it was almost inevitable, and certainly fitting, that one of these fine locomotives should capture for all time the World Speed Record for Steam Traction.

Chapter and verse has already been written about the A4s and their exploits, so within the pages of this book we have simply tried to compile a fitting pictorial tribute illustrating each engine in varying guises. Our grateful thanks are offered once again to fellow photographers who have so kindly allowed us to use their pictures, and to Lesley and Anne who typed the manuscript.

SUMMARY

BR No.	Orig. No.	First 1946 No.	Second 1946 No.	Built	Maker	Works No.	Original Name	Later Name	Double Chimney	Withdrawn
60001	7/48	4500		1 11/46	4/1938	Doncaster	1873	Garganey	Sir Ronald Matthews (3/39)	4/58	10/64
60002	5/48	4499		2 10/46	4/1938	Doncaster	1872	Pochard	Sir Murrough Wilson (4/39)	7/57	5/64
60003	3/49	4494		3 9/46	8/1937	Doncaster	1859	Osprey	Andrew K. McCosh (10/42)	7/57	12/62
60004	5/48	4462		4 8/46	11/1937	Doncaster	1864	Great Snipe	William Whitelaw (7/41)	12/57	7/66
60005	7/48	4901		5 8/46	6/1938	Doncaster	1875	Capercaillie	Charles H. Newton (9/42) / Sir Charles Newton (6/43)	New	3/64
60006	12/48	4466	605 1/46	6 5/46	1/1938	Doncaster	1868	Herring Gull	Sir Ralph Wedgwood (1/44)	9/57	9/65
60007	3/48	4498		7 1/47	11/1937	Doncaster	1863	Sir Nigel Gresley		12/57	2/66
60008	10/48	4496		8 11/46	9/1937	Doncaster	1861	Golden Shuttle	Dwight D. Eisenhower (9/45)	8/58	7/63
60009	5/48	4488		9 1/47	6/1937	Doncaster	1853	Union of South Africa		11/58	6/66
60010	10/48	4489		10 5/46	5/1937	Doncaster	1854	Woodcock	Dominion of Canada (6/37)	12/57	5/65
60011	3/49	4490		11 11/46	6/1937	Doncaster	1855	Empire of India		1/58	5/64
60012	5/48	4491		12 1/47	6/1937	Doncaster	1856	Commonwealth of Australia		7/58	8/64
60013	5/49	4492		13 8/46	6/1937	Doncaster	1857	Dominion of New Zealand		7/58	4/63
60014	6/49	2509		14 6/46	9/1935	Doncaster	1818	Silver Link		10/57	12/62
60015	12/48	2510		15 9/46	9/1935	Doncaster	1819	Quicksilver		8/57	4/63
60016	6/48	2511		16 11/46	11/1935	Doncaster	1821	Silver King		6/57	3/65
60017	4/49	2512		17 9/46	12/1935	Doncaster	1823	Silver Fox		5/57	10/63
60018	10/48	4463		18 9/46	12/1937	Doncaster	1865	Sparrow Hawk		10/57	6/63
60019	10/48	4464		19 8/46	12/1937	Doncaster	1866	Bittern		9/57	9/66
60020	10/48	4465		20 9/46	12/1937	Doncaster	1867	Guillemot		11/57	3/64
60021	9/48	4467		21 5/46	2/1938	Doncaster	1869	Wild Swan		4/58	10/63
60022	9/49	4468		22 9/46	3/1938	Doncaster	1870	Mallard		New	4/63
60023	3/48	4482		23 11/46	12/1936	Doncaster	1847	Golden Eagle		9/58	10/64
60024	6/48	4483	585 3/46	24 5/46	12/1936	Doncaster	1848	Kingfisher		8/58	9/66
60025	1/50	4484		25 5/46	2/1937	Doncaster	1849	Falcon		9/58	10/63
60026	9/49	4485	587 4/46	26 5/46	2/1937	Doncaster	1850	Kestrel	Miles Beevor (11/47)	8/57	12/65
60027	6/48	4486	588 3/46	27 5/46	3/1937	Doncaster	1851	Merlin		2/58	9/65
60028	6/48	4487		28 11/46	4/1937	Doncaster	1852	Sea Eagle	Walter K. Whigham (10/47)	11/57	12/62
60029	7/48	4493		29 5/46	7/1937	Doncaster	1858	Woodcock		10/58	10/63
60030	7/48	4495		30 11/46	8/1937	Doncaster	1860	Great Snipe	Golden Fleece (9/37)	5/58	12/62
60031	6/48	4497		31 5/46	10/1937	Doncaster	1862	Golden Plover		3/58	10/65
60032	6/49	4900		32 11/46	5/1938	Doncaster	1874	Gannet		11/58	10/63
60033	4/48	4902		33 10/46	6/1938	Doncaster	1876	Seagull		New	12/62
60034	3/48	4903		34 11/46	7/1938	Doncaster	1877	Peregrine	Lord Faringdon (3/48)	New	8/66
—		4469		—	3/1938	Doncaster	1871	Gadwall	Sir Ralph Wedgwood (3/39)	—	6/42

Cover illustration:
No. 60021 *Wild Swan* at Leeds Central in March 1961.
Gavin Morrison

First published 1985
This impression 1999

ISBN 0 86093 354 7

Published by Oxford Publishing Co

an imprint of Ian Allan Publishing Ltd, Terminal House, Shepperton, Surrey TW17 8AS.
Printed by Ian Allan Printing Ltd, Riverdene Business Park, Hersham, Surrey KT12 4RG.

Code: 9904/A1

60001 SIR RONALD MATTHEWS

Plate 1 (Left): Delivered in April 1938 as No. 4500 *Garganey*, it is seen the following month, when still almost brand new heading an 'up' express at Low Fell.

W. B. Greenfield, NELPG Collection

Plate 2 (Above): On 6th June 1940, and by now having been renamed *Sir Ronald Matthews*, it is seen again near Low Fell heading an 'up' express. It is still looking resplendent in its original LNER Garter blue livery which it retained until being painted black during the war years.

W. B. Greenfield, NELPG Collection

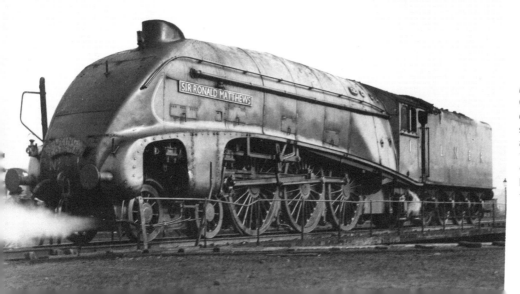

Plate 3 (Left): From the summer of 1946, Garter blue livery was reinstated to all A4s, combined with the new 1946 numbers. It is seen in this livery standing on the turntable at Grantham on 6th October 1947, with the 'cut-out' metal letters and number clearly visible on the tender and cab side. This locomotive was allocated to Gateshead from new until withdrawal in 1964.

T. G. Hepburn, Rail Archive Stephenson

Plate 4 (Above): On 14th August 1958, with its British Railways number and standard dark green livery with orange and black lining, it is seen passing Durham with a southbound express of all maroon coaching stock.

D. M. C. Hepburne-Scott,
Rail Archive Stephenson

Plate 5 (Left): In May 1960 No. 60001 *Sir Ronald Matthews* is passing Greenwood heading an express from King's Cross to Newcastle. The engine is in a filthy external condition, which at that time was so often typical of Gateshead engines.

D. Cross

Plate 6 (Below): In this picture of No. 60001 leaving York on 1st September 1962, with the 10.40 King's Cross – Newcastle express, the chime whistle directly in front of the double chimney appears to be badly bent.

John Whiteley

Plate 7 (Right): The chime whistle can also be seen to be bent in this picture taken on 2nd June 1962, of No. 60001 passing Croft Spa heading the 17.10 Newcastle to King's Cross express. At this period this train was given a booked time of forty minutes for the forty-four miles from Darlington to York.

R. H. Leslie

Plate 8 (Left): With clouds of thick black smoke pouring forth from its double chimney, all does not seem well on the footplate as it approaches Stoke Tunnel on 7th July 1962, with the 'down' Niddrie goods, which was often worked by an A4 in this period.

Gavin Morrison

Plate 9 (Below): On Sunday 20th October 1963, No. 60001 *Sir Ronald Matthews* is between duties at York alongside Gresley V2 No. 60967. Unlike the first 21 engines which were all originally coupled to corridor tenders, *Sir Ronald Matthews* was one of the last 14 to be delivered, all of these being initially coupled to streamlined non-corridor tenders. Through the years, tenders were continually being exchanged, but this particular A4 was one of seven, all of which were allocated to Newcastle depots, which were never coupled to corridor tenders.

Gavin Morrison

60002
SIR MURROUGH WILSON

Plate 10 (Right): No. 4499 *Pochard* is seen at Gateshead Motive Power Depot on 15th April 1938, shortly after being built. The handle which was used to open the streamlined front casing outwards, giving access to the smokebox door, can be seen on the casing above the cylinder.

W. B. Greenfield, NELPG Collection

Plate 11 (Left): This locomotive was renamed *Sir Murrough Wilson* after only one year, and apart from a brief spell of a few weeks in 1943 when it was allocated to King's Cross, it was always allocated to Gateshead. This was another of the Newcastle based A4s which was never coupled to a corridor tender, with the result that it never participated in the non-stop running between London and Edinburgh. On 14th May 1960, it is seen just North of Newark heading the 'down' 'Heart of Midlothian'.

T. Boustead

Plate 12 (Above): The Gateshead A4s rarely shared the limelight with their Scottish or Southern counterparts on the more glamorous workings, and this is typified in this picture of No. 60002 *Sir Murrough Wilson* heading a northbound freight at Monkton Hall on 7th July 1962.

D. Cross

Plate 13 (Left): On 8th February 1964, only a few months before withdrawal, it is seen inside Heaton Shed. In this view, the modified opening arrangement to the front casing can be seen, with the lower door now supported on chains.

Gavin Morrison

60003 ANDREW K. McCOSH

Plate 14 (Right): No. 4494 was originally named *Osprey* and was one of nine A4s, Nos. 4482-7 and Nos. 4493-5, turned out in lined green livery with shaded gold numbers and letters. It is seen in this livery at Hadley Wood in 1938 heading an 'up' Leeds express.

C. R. L. Coles

Plate 15 (Left): In 1937 it was decided to standardise on Garter blue livery for all the A4s, and No. 4494 was the final A4 in green livery, being repainted Garter blue in October 1938. After a period in black livery during the war, it was repainted Garter blue in June 1947, having been renamed *Andrew K. McCosh* in October 1942, after a high ranking official of the LNER. It is seen here as No. 3 leaving Welwyn North Tunnel heading the 'up' 'Flying Scotsman' in 1947.

F. R. Hebron, Rail Archive Stephenson

Plate 16 (Below): No. 60003 is seen after Nationalisation, in 1949, approaching Hatfield with the 'down' 'Yorkshire Pullman'.

F. R. Hebron, Rail Archive Stephenson

Plate 17 (Left): After Nationalisation, with the exception of a few months in 1957, No. 60003 was allocated to King's Cross. It is seen here on 10th June 1950, having just been repainted in BR blue livery, emerging from Peascliffe Tunnel with the 'up' 'Capitals Limited'.

J. P. Wilson

Plate 18 (Above): The 'Capitals Limited' was a non-stop service between London and Edinburgh, and in this fine picture No. 60003 is seen at the head of the 'down' train making a vigorous assault of Holloway Bank.

J. C. Flemons

Plate 19 (Left): On 17th April 1952, by now in BR dark green livery with orange and black lining, it is leaving Essendine with a morning Grantham – King's Cross train.

P. H. Wells

Plate 20 (Right): Having now been rebuilt with a double chimney, No. 60003 is passing Pilmoor heading a King's Cross – Newcastle express on 16th August 1959.

Gavin Morrison

Plate 21 (Left): The 'up' 'Junior Scotsman' has just emerged from Stoke Tunnel behind No. 60003 on 21st July 1962.

Gavin Morrison

Plate 22 (Below): Resting between duties at Doncaster on 17th June 1962. With the onset of dieselisation on the Eastern Region, No. 60003 was one of five King's Cross A4s withdrawn on 29th December 1962.

Gavin Morrison

Plate 23 (Below): This picture clearly shows the smokebox door which has been exposed by opening the front casing. The upper section is supported by metal brackets and the smaller lower portion, which was originally also held by metal brackets, is now supported by chains.

Gavin Morrison

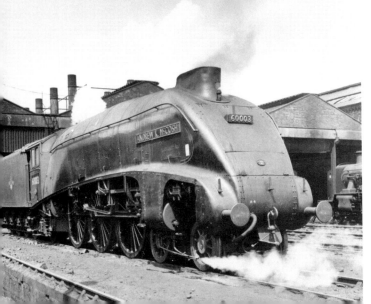

60004
WILLIAM
WHITELAW

Plate 24 (Right): The first batch of four A4s (Nos. 2509-12) were built for working the 'Silver Jubilee', and were all given appropriate names (see *Plate 85*). The names originally selected for the remainder of the A4s were of British birds noted for swift flight, although in the end several of these proposed names were altered before the locomotives in question were delivered. No. 4462 was originally named *Great Snipe*, and in this photograph it is seen in its original Garter blue livery at Grantham heading a 'down' express in the late 1930s.

T. G. Hepburn, Rail Archive Stephenson

Plate 25 (Below): Shortly after Nationalisation it is seen as No. 60004 *William Whitelaw* passing Harringay heading the 'down' 'Capitals Limited'. During 1939 a decision had been made to honour some of the higher ranking officials of the LNER by naming locomotives after them, and in July 1941 this A4 was named after a Chairman of the LNER. When it was renamed, it was transferred to Haymarket and given a corridor tender, enabling it to participate in the non-stop workings between King's Cross and Edinburgh. During the War, to facilitate easier maintenance, it was decided to remove the skirting from both behind and in front of the cylinders. This was the first A4 to be dealt with, in June 1941, but when it returned to traffic in July a modified form of skirting had been replaced in front of the cylinders. This was duly removed in October 1942, and by this date the skirtings had been completely removed from all the other A4s.

F. R. Hebron, Rail Archive Stephenson

Plate 26 (Right): After this locomotive was transferred to Haymarket, in 1941, it remained in Scotland for the rest of its life, having spells at Haymarket and Aberdeen Ferryhill. On 1st September 1956, whilst still allocated to Haymarket, it is seen approaching Edinburgh through Princess Street Gardens heading an express from Glasgow.

R. H. Leslie

Plate 27 (Left): In 1953, in honour of the new Queen, 'The Capitals Limited' was renamed 'The Elizabethan', and on 17th May 1953, it is seen awaiting departure from Edinburgh Waverley.

P. H. Wells

Plate 28 (Below): On 19th September 1965, No. 60004 *William Whitelaw* is seen after arrival at Leeds with a return RCTS rail tour. By this time, all the surviving A4s were allocated to either Aberdeen Ferryhill or Glasgow St. Rollox, participating mainly on services between Glasgow and Aberdeen on the former Caledonian main line.

John Whiteley

60005
SIR CHARLES NEWTON

Plate 29 (Right): No. 4901 was *Capercaillie* until being renamed after the Chief General Manager of the LNER in 1942. It was one of the last three A4s to be built, Nos. 4901-3, all of which were built with a double blast-pipe and chimney. This arrangement having been fitted to No. 4468 *Mallard* earlier in 1938. Surprisingly, a similar double blast-pipe and chimney arrangement was not fitted to the remainder of the A4s for some 20 years or so.

W. B. Greenfield, NELPG Collection

Plate 30 (Left): *Capercaillie* leaving Newcastle Central on 12th August 1939, heading an 'up' express. Until being transferred to Scotland for the last few months of its working life, this locomotive was always allocated to Gateshead.

W. B. Greenfield, NELPG Collection

Plate 31 (Right): No. 60005 was one of the seven A4s never to be paired with a corridor tender, and on 23rd July 1960, it is leaving Grantham with a 'down' Newcastle express.

T. Boustead

Plate 32 (Above): No. 60005 *Sir Charles Newton* is climbing towards Stoke Tunnel, near Little Ponton, on 11th June 1950, heading an 'up' Scottish express. After Nationalisation, various liveries were tried with the A4s. From May 1949, for a brief period until the introduction of standard BR dark green in August 1951, the A4s were painted dark blue with black and white lining. It is seen in this livery with the first style of Lion and Wheel emblem on the tender which replaced the lettering 'British Railways'.

T. G. Hepburn, Rail Archive Stephenson

Plate 33 (Below): In a filthy condition, so often associated with Gateshead engines, No. 60005 leaves York on 10th September 1960, heading the 10.35 Newcastle – King's Cross. This was one of four Gateshead A4s which were transferred to Scotland after the end of the 1963 summer services, having been made redundant on the East Coast main line by new diesel locomotives. However, it only had a brief spell at both St. Margaret's and Aberdeen, being withdrawn in March 1964.

R. H. Leslie

60006
SIR RALPH
WEDGWOOD

Plate 34 (Right): No. 4466 *Herring Gull* was another A4 originally given the name of a bird, but subsequently renamed after an official of the LNER. This followed the scrapping of No. 4469, which had also been renamed *Sir Ralph Wedgwood*, but which was destroyed following air raid damage sustained at York in April 1942. It is seen shortly before departure from Newcastle Central early in 1938.

W. B. Greenfield, NELPG Collection

Plate 35 (Left): Having been renamed *Sir Ralph Wedgwood* in January 1944, it is seen heading a 'down' Newcastle express at Hadley Wood in 1946. It is carrying the Number 605, and was one of only four A4s ever to carry numbers which had been prepared as part of the 1943 renumbering scheme. No sooner had these four A4s been renumbered than it was decided to renumber the whole class numerically from No. 1. Unlined black livery had been implemented from late 1941 as an austerity war-time measure, and several merely had the letters 'NE' painted on the tender, as can be seen in this picture.

C. R. L. Coles

Plate 36 (Right): On 9th July 1955, No. 60006 is seen leaving Essendine heading a 'down' express. By this time it has been repainted in standard BR dark green, but has not yet been rebuilt with a double chimney.

P. H. Wells

Plate 37 (Above): From July 1950 until June 1954, No. 60006 was coupled to a corridor tender whilst allocated to King's Cross. In this picture it is seen near Hatfield in 1952 heading the 'up' 'Flying Scotsman'.

F. R. Hebron, Rail Archive Stephenson

Plate 38 (Left): On 7th March 1962, by now fitted with a double chimney and coupled to a streamlined non-corridor tender, No. 60006 leaves Leeds Central with the 12.30 to King's Cross.

Gavin Morrison

Plate 39 (Right): In June 1963, No. 60006 was one of 11 A4s transferred to New England when King's Cross top shed was closed. Several of these were withdrawn shortly afterwards, but No. 60006 was one of five A4s then transferred to Scotland, initially to St. Margaret's and subsequently to Ferryhill, from where it was withdrawn in September 1965. In this picture, taken at Perth on 20th April 1965, it is standing on the West Coast Postal combined with the 17.10 Perth to Carstairs train. This photograph was taken not long after the infamous Great Train Robbery, and understandably at this period, the authorities were rather sensitive towards photography of this train.

John Whiteley

60007 SIR NIGEL GRESLEY

Plate 40 (Right): No. 4498 was the one hundreth Gresley Pacific to be built, and it was felt appropriate that this particular locomotive be named after its designer. Ten other A4s were subsequently named after Directors and officials of the Company. This was the last of the second batch of A4s comprising 17 locomotives, 10 of which, including No. 4498, were coupled to corridor tenders which had previously been coupled to 'A1' and 'A3' Pacifics. These second-hand corridor tenders could be distinguished by the external beading along the top edge of the tender, as seen in the three photographs on this page. No. 4498 is seen here emerging from Potters Bar Tunnel heading the 16.15 King's Cross – Grantham semi-fast on 13th May 1939.   *J. G. Dewing*

Plate 41 (Left): The 'Coronation' was the second LNER streamlined train. It started operating on 3rd July 1937, between King's Cross and Edinburgh, leaving King's Cross at 16.00 with one stop at York, and leaving Edinburgh at 16.30 with one stop at Newcastle. A stop at Newcastle was subsequently added to the schedule of the 'down' train. On 11th May 1939, No. 4498 is heading the 'down' 'Coronation' near Lamesley.

W. B. Greenfield, NELPG Collection

Plate 42 (Below): No. 4498 was not one of the five engines which were originally chosen to haul the 'Coronation', but it was nevertheless finished in a similar fashion with stainless steel edging to the bottom of the skirting and tender. In January 1939 it was also given stainless steel cut-out numbers and letters, but in this photograph, taken in 1938, it still has its original painted numbers and letters. It is seen at Ganwick in 1938 heading the 'down' 'Flying Scotsman'.

C. R. L. Coles

Plate 43 (Above): On 14th June 1962, No. 60007 *Sir Nigel Gresley* is heading the 'down' 'Talisman', north of Finsbury Park. This was an afternoon service between London and Edinburgh with an engine change at Newcastle.

P. H. Groom

Plate 44 (right): No. 60007 was another King's Cross A4 which was transferred to New England in June 1963, and subsequently transferred to Scotland where it worked from Ferryhill until being withdrawn in February 1966. In this photograph, taken on a very wet day in August 1964, it is leaving Stirling heading the 'up' 'Bon Accord', which ran between Aberdeen and Glasgow. By the look of the front end, it has hit a large feathered object en-route.

John Whiteley

Plate 45 (Below): After *Sir Nigel Gresley* had been withdrawn, it was purchased by the A4 Locomotive Society Limited and restored in working condition to Garter blue livery, which of course it never carried with a double chimney. In this photograph taken in May 1967 it is passing Beattock heading a Carlisle – Perth parcels train on its way to Scotland for a special working.

D. Cross

Plates 46 and 47: Two pictures on this page showing *Sir Nigel Gresley* on BR steam hauled excursions.

Above: Accelerating away from Settle Junction on 6th February 1982, *Sir Nigel Gresley* is en-route from Carnforth to Hellifield heading the 'Cumbrian Mountain Pullman'.

Below: Approaching Blea Moor with the northbound 'Cumbrian Mountain Pullman' on 28th November 1981.

Both John Whiteley

60008
DWIGHT
D. EISENHOWER

Plate 48 (Right): In 1939 the 'down' 'West Riding Limited' is passing Potters Bar behind No. 4496 *Golden Shuttle*. This was the third of the LNER streamlined trains, which went into service on 27th September 1937, between Bradford, Leeds and King's Cross. Nos. 4495 and 4496 were selected to work these trains and were given names appropriate to the Yorkshire woollen trade together with a trim, as previously described in *Plate 42*.

C. R. L. Coles

Plate 49 (Left): No. 4496 was renamed in 1945, not after an Officer of the Company, but after the Supreme Commander of the Allied Forces during the latter part of the war. It had been repainted in LNER blue in September 1945. In this picture taken at Grantham on 11th June 1946, the stainless steel cut out numbers and letters on the cab and tender sides are clearly seen.

T. G. Hepburn, Rail Archive Stephenson

Plate 50 (Below): Also in 1946, it is seen nearing Potters Bar with an express from Leeds, whilst allocated to Grantham.

F. R. Hebron, Rail Archive Stephenson

Plate 51 (Above): *Dwight D. Eisenhower* had been coupled to a corridor tender from new, but in April 1957 this was exchanged for a streamlined non-corridor tender. It is seen here on 5th August 1962, heading an 'up' express near Hitchin.

D. M. C. Hepburne-Scott, Rail Archive Stephenson

Plate 52 (Right): No. 60008 is racing south in this photograph taken near Pilmoor on 16th August 1959, whilst it was heading an Edinburgh – King's Cross express.

Gavin Morrison

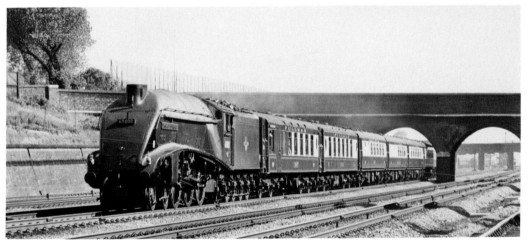

Plate 53 (Left): On 14th June 1962, No. 60008 is seen north of Finsbury Park heading the 'down' 'Tees-Tyne Pullman'. At this period it was allocated to King's Cross and booked to a regular crew in the top link for prestige turns such as this.

P. H. Groom

Plate 54 (Right): Copley Hill Shed, Leeds on 19th March 1963, showing No. 60008 going on shed and flanked by Thompson Class B1 No. 61016 *Inyala*. This was another King's Cross A4 which was transferred to New England in June 1963, when Top Shed closed, but it was withdrawn the following month and the locomotive is now preserved in North America.

John Whiteley

60009 UNION OF SOUTH AFRICA

Plate 55 (Left): No. 4488 Union of South Africa was one of five A4s (Nos. 4488-92) specially prepared for working the streamlined 'Coronation' high speed train. The 'Coronation' was an eight coach train, plus beaver tail observation car which was used on the summer services. The five engines selected for these services were all painted in a matching Garter blue livery with cut-out metal numbers. No. 4488 is seen heading the 'up' 'Coronation' near Low Fell on 29th June 1938.

W. B. Greenfield, NELPG Collection

Plate 56 (Right): In this picture, Union of South Africa is seen standing inside Newcastle Central early in 1939, heading the 'down' 'Flying Scotsman'. The five A4s originally selected for working the 'Coronation' were all appropriately given names of countries in the British Empire, and hand painted coats of arms of the appropriate country were fixed to each side of the cab underneath the numbers, as can be seen in this picture. The picture also shows the stainless steel edging strip to the skirting.

W. B. Greenfield, NELPG Collection

Plate 57 (Below): No. 60009 is passing Grantshouse on 23rd August 1960, heading the 09.30 Glasgow (Queen Street) – King's Cross. This engine was one of the Scottish faithfuls, and in common with the other Haymarket A4s, was invariably kept in extremely good mechanical and external condition.

R. H. Leslie

Plate 58 (Above): The Haymarket A4s were not regular visitors to London, other than on the non-stop workings, but in this picture No. 60009 is heading the up 'Northumbrian' at Ganwick in July 1960.

D. Cross

Plate 59 (Above): *Union of South Africa* was allocated to Haymarket from new until being transferred to Aberdeen Ferryhill in May 1962. It had the distinction, however, of being the last A4 to work a train out of King's Cross, when on 24th October 1964, it hauled an RCTS/SLS Special to Newcastle and back. This picture was taken at Perth Motive Power Depot on 6th July 1965, and shows *Union of South Africa* in the company of a 'Britannia' Pacific, a Stanier Class 5 and also No. 60026 *Miles Beevor*. John Whiteley

Plate 60 (Below): During the mid 1960s, in common with other Ferryhill A4s, No. 60009 worked the three hour services between Aberdeen and Glasgow. It is seen here leaving Perth on 5th June 1965, heading the 'up' 'Grampian'. No. 60009 was withdrawn in June 1966, and was the A4 to achieve the highest mileage, having attained 1, 643, 728 miles in June 1962, and probably totalling over 1, 800, 000 miles when it was finally withdrawn. John Whiteley

Plate 61 (Above): No. 60009 was the last A4 to receive a general repair at Doncaster, and after its withdrawal, was purchased by a group of businessmen headed by Mr John Cameron. It was stationed on the Lochty Private Railway and is now preserved in main line running order, happily in BR livery. This photograph shows it passing Haymarket on 14th April 1979, with a special to Aberdeen. The rectangular plate depicting a springbok, which was placed on one side of the engine only, in April 1954, can be seen.   *John Whiteley*

Plate 62 (Below): In action again, this time on 6th September 1980, leaving Aberdeen under the famous signal gantries, with a returning excursion to Edinburgh.

John Whiteley

60010 DOMINION OF CANADA

Plate 63 (Right): No. 4489 was originally to have been named *Buzzard*, but when it was put into traffic early in May 1937, it was named *Woodcock*. For about two weeks it ran in shop grey livery with green painted coupled wheels, but it soon returned to Doncaster, and towards the end of May emerged in Garter blue livery, renamed *Dominion of Canada* having been chosen to haul the 'Coronation' streamlined express. Here it is seen taking water at Newcastle, in June 1938, heading the 'down' 'Flying Scotsman'.

W. B. Greenfield, NELPG Collection

Plate 64 (Left): In 1947, it is seen as renumbered 10, still in wartime black livery, but with cut-out numbers and letters LNER on the tender. It is heading a 'down' Leeds express near Welwyn South.

F. R. Hebron, Rail Archive Stephenson

Plate 65 (Below): On 12th March 1957, No. 60010 leaves Cambridge with a slow for King's Cross. This A4 was unique in carrying a bell mounted directly in front of its chimney. This bell was presented by the Canadian Pacific Railway Company and was fixed in position in March 1938. It remained until November 1957 when it was removed to allow the fitting of a double chimney.

D. M. C. Hepburne-Scott, Rail Archive Stephenson

Plate 66 (Right): On 19th July 1958, now fitted with a double chimney, No. 60010 is leaving Grantham with the 10.35 Newcastle – King's Cross.

P. H. Groom

Plate 67 (Below): Apart from a few weeks at Grantham in 1957, No. 60010 spent all its working life allocated to King's Cross until closure in 1963, when it was transferred to New England, and shortly afterwards to Aberdeen Ferryhill. Here it is seen on 24th June 1961, passing Welwyn Garden City, heading the 10.28 King's Cross – York.

R. H. Leslie

Plate 68 (Below): On 21st August 1964, now allocated to Aberdeen Ferryhill, it is nearing Gleneagles, heading the West Coast Postal, a regular A4 working at this time from Aberdeen, to either Perth or Carstairs. In this picture it is in rather run down external condition, rather untypical of the condition in which the A4s were kept at Ferryhill during their last few years of service.

John Whiteley

Plate 69 (Below): Dominion of Canada is seen on shed at Glasgow St. Rollox on 31st March 1964. The 'cods mouth' is open, revealing the inner smokebox door. No. 60010 was withdrawn in May 1965, due to the poor condition of its boiler. Over a year later it was restored externally at Crewe Works, after which it was shipped to Canada for static display.

Gavin Morrison

60011 EMPIRE OF INDIA

Plate 70 (Right): No. 4490 *Empire of India* enters Newcastle in August 1938 heading the 'up' 'Coronation', the service for which it was originally intended and appropriately turned out with all the various embelishments. Only King's Cross and Haymarket engines were rostered for these through workings, and although No. 4490 was initially allocated to King's Cross, it was transferred to Haymarket in March 1938, where it remained until being transferred to Aberdeen Ferryhill in June 1962.

W. B. Greenfield, NELPG Collection

Plate 71 (Left): Another picture of No. 4490 heading the 'up' 'Coronation', this time taken on 14th July 1938, at Low Fell.

W. B. Greenfield, NELPG Collection

Plate 72 (Below): This picture shows No. 60011 *Empire of India* climbing out of Leeds, running in on a Leeds – Doncaster local, having just had its last major overhaul at Doncaster. Not long after this overhaul, it was transferred from Haymarket to Ferryhill, but in this picture taken on 5th June 1962, it can still be seen displaying a Haymarket shed code beneath the front number.

Gavin Morrison

Plate 73 (Right): No. 60011 is again seen on a running-in turn, this time on 30th May 1959, heading a southbound train of coal just south of Grantham. Originally the cab roofs of the A4s were fitted with one central ventilator, but this was soon found to be insufficient, and two additional ventilators, one at each side above each seat, were fitted from 1937, following trials with No. 2509 in 1936. The open ventilators can clearly be seen in this picture.

T. Boustead

Plate 74 (Left): No. 60011 is again seen on a mundane freight duty, this time passing Grantshouse on 23rd August 1960 heading a 'down' coal train.

R. H. Leslie

Plate 75 (Right): On 2nd March 1963, now having been transferred to Ferryhill, No. 60011 is passing Bridge of Allan with a 3 hour Aberdeen – Glasgow express.

D. Cross

60012
COMMONWEALTH OF AUSTRALIA

Plate 76 (Left): Also selected for use on the 'Coronation' services, No. 4491 was turned out in Garter blue livery, named *Commonwealth of Australia* and provided with the appropriate coat of arms for the cab-sides. Apart from working the 'Coronation', the Haymarket A4s often worked to Glasgow, Dundee and Perth at this period, and in later years worked through to Aberdeen. In this picture, taken on 5th September 1938, it has just crossed the Forth Bridge heading the 14.10 train from Edinburgh Waverley to Perth.

T. G. Hepburn, Rail Archive Stephenson

Plate 77 (Below): *Commonwealth of Australia* was allocated to Haymarket from new until 1963. On 19th May 1956, it is emerging from Mound Tunnel, shortly after leaving Edinburgh Waverley with an express for Aberdeen. It is passing another equally clean Haymarket A4, No. 60024 *Kingfisher* which appears to have been very well coaled and is waiting to reverse into Waverley Station.

J. P. Wilson

Plate 78 (Above): On 11th September 1958, No. 60012 leaves Stoke Tunnel heading the 'up' 'Elizabethan', with still a remarkably good supply of coal left in the tender, bearing in mind the locomotive has worked through from Edinburgh. *T. G. Hepburn, Rail Archive Stephenson*

Plate 79 (Below): Four A4s, Nos. 60003/8/10/30, were allocated to Grantham from April 1957 until September 1957 for use on the summer services, but with this exception, all thirty-four A4s were allocated to only three sheds between 1951 and 1961, namely King's Cross, Gateshead and Haymarket. Haymarket A4s were regular performers on the 'Elizabethan', and No. 60012 is seen again on the southbound train, this time in August 1958, nearing Newark. *T. Boustead*

60013 DOMINION OF NEW ZEALAND

Plate 80 (Above): No. 4492 *Dominion of New Zealand* was the last of the five A4s selected for use on the 'Coronation', and turned out in matching Garter blue livery. In this June 1938 picture, however, it is departing from King's Cross heading the 'down' 'Silver Jubilee'. This train had been introduced in 1935 between Newcastle and King's Cross with one intermediate stop at Darlington. The striking silver-grey livery of the coaches can be seen in this picture, together with the rubber fairings concealing the gap between the coaches and also the extended lower bodyside panelling between the bogies to reduce wind resistance. *W. B. Greenfield, NELPG Collection*

Plate 81 (Below): The 'Tees-Tyne Pullman' was the post-war equivalent of the 'Silver Jubilee', and the 'up' train is seen passing Grantham South Box behind No. 60013 on 28th March 1951.

J. P. Wilson

Plate 82 (Right): In its last year with a single chimney, No. 60013 is seen nearing Essendine, on 15th August 1957, heading the 'down' 'Flying Scotsman'. Having originally been paired with a corridor tender, between 1950 and 1955 it was coupled to a streamlined non-corridor tender, reverting back to a corridor tender in April 1955.

P. H. Wells

Plate 83 (Left): A heavy Edinburgh – King's Cross express of all maroon stock is accelerated away from York on 1st September 1962. In May 1939 No. 60013 had been fitted with a New Zealand Government railway whistle which was larger and pitched lower than the standard chime whistle. The size of this larger whistle is evident in this picture.

John Whiteley

Plate 84 (Right): On 5th September 1959, it is making a seemingly effortless ascent to Stoke Tunnel from Grantham, seen passing Little Ponton, heading the 'up' 'Flying Scotsman'. Withdrawn from service in April 1963, when allocated to King's Cross, No. 60013 was one of 14 A4s, (including No. 4469 which suffered war damage), which were cut up at Doncaster.

Gavin Morrison

60014 SILVER LINK

Plate 85 (Left): No. 2509 *Silver Link* is seen at King's Cross on 14th September 1935, having arrived brand-new from Doncaster the previous day. Not only was the streamlined appearance so unconventional, but the livery in three contrasting shades of grey was arguably the most striking ever to adorn a steam locomotive. The front of the smokebox casing was painted dark charcoal grey, the side skirtings and frames were battleship grey and the remainder of the engine cab and tender was silver grey with no lining-out whatsoever.

F. G. Carrier

Plate 86 (Right): In 1936 No. 2509 is leaving Grantham heading an 'up' express. This was the first A4, and together with the next three, Nos. 2510-12, they all went into traffic in this striking grey livery, with their names, all following the 'silver' theme, painted on the side of the boiler casings. For about nine months none of these first four A4s carried numbers at the front end.

T. G. Hepburn, Rail Archive Stephenson

Plate 87 (Below): On the service for which it was intended, No. 2509 enters Darlington heading the 'up' 'Silver Jubilee' on 21st June 1937. In this picture the three contrasting shades of grey on the locomotive show up well, particularly the silver grey of the wheels. The 'up' train left Newcastle at 10.00 with a stop at Darlington, reaching King's Cross at 14.00. The return train left King's Cross at 17.30, reaching Newcastle at 21.30 after a stop at Darlington. Initially it comprised seven coaches, but was soon increased to eight as a result of its popularity.

W. B. Greenfield, NELPG Collection

Plate 88 (Above): Following the introduction of the 'Coronation' streamlined train in the summer of 1937 hauled by A4s in matching Garter blue livery the decision was taken later in 1937 to repaint the A4s, which were then in both silver grey and also green livery, in a standardised Garter blue livery. When the 'silver' A4s were repainted during 1937 and 1938 they were each provided with nameplates to replace names which had previously been painted on the boiler casing. In this condition No. 2509 is seen heading an 'up' Newcastle express at Potters Bar in 1938.

C. R. L. Coles

Plate 89 (Right): On 18th April 1938, No. 2509 is seen near Raskelf heading a 'down' express. It should be noted in both this and the above picture that the number of the locomotive is now carried in the standard fashion at the front.

T. G. Hepburn, Rail Archive Stephenson

Plate 90 (Left): Having just been restored to LNER blue livery after its war-time black, and at the same time having been renumbered 14, Silver Link leaves Grantham with an 'up' slow on 30th August 1946. The nameplates of both Silver Link and also Quicksilver differed from all the other A4 nameplates in having rounded corners as opposed to squared corners. The rounded corners of the nameplate can be seen in this picture (see also Plate 96).

T. G. Hepburn, Rail Archive Stephenson

Plate 91 (Left): Now sporting BR green livery with the early lion and wheel emblem on the tender, No. 60014 is working hard on the climb to Stoke Tunnel heading the 'up' 'Flying Scotsman' on 18th June 1955.

J. P. Wilson

Plate 92 (Below): A panoramic view of King's Cross sees No. 60014 about to plunge into Gasworks Tunnel heading the 'down' 'Yorkshire Pullman' on 9th July 1955.

*D. M. C. Hepburne-Scott,
Rail Archive Stephenson*

Plate 93 (Left): In immaculate condition, and now with double chimney, it is seen racing past Abbots Ripton with the 'down' 'Tees Thames Express' on 21st July 1961, overtaking Austerity No. 90240 on the 'down' slow line. How fitting it would have been if this historic A4 had been preserved. Sadly, it was one of five Eastern Region A4s at King's Cross withdrawn on 29th December 1962, and subsequently cut up at Doncaster.

R. H. Leslie

60015
QUICKSILVER

Plate 94 (Left): When the 'Silver Jubilee' streamlined train went into service, No. 2509 *Silver Link*, was the only A4 to have been completed, and worked the train for the first two weeks until No. 2510 *Quicksilver* had been delivered. In this July 1937 picture, No. 2510 is approaching New Barnet, heading the 'down' 'Silver Jubilee'. It is in its original grey livery but has had its number painted on the front.

J. P. Wilson

Plate 95 (Right): No. 2510 was repainted in Garter blue in May 1938, at which time nameplates were attached at the front of the boiler casings. In July 1938 it is seen passing Low Fell, heading the 'up' 'Coronation' on its scheduled six hour run from Edinburgh to King's Cross, including one stop at Newcastle. This was an even more demanding schedule than that of the 'Silver Jubilee' bearing in mind it was a slightly heavier load over a considerably greater distance, necessitating an average speed of just over 62m.p.h. between Edinburgh and Newcastle, and 68m.p.h. for the 268.3 miles between Newcastle and King's Cross.

W. B. Greenfield, NELPG Collection

Plate 96 (Below): Standing at the head of an 'up' express at Darlington on 9th June 1939, *Quicksilver* is in Garter blue livery with the rounded corners of the nameplate clearly visible.

T. G. Hepburn, Rail Archive Stephenson

Plate 97 (Top): On 29th August 1958, No. 60015 passes beneath the impressive signal gantry at High Dyke as it approaches Stoke Tunnel, heading an 'up' express.

T. G. Hepburn, Rail Archive Stephenson

Plate 98 (Centre): In this picture, taken in July 1959, it has just emerged from Hadley Wood South Tunnel at Greenwood, heading an 'up' sleeping car express.

D. Cross

Plate 99 (Left): *Quicksilver* was only to see a few more weeks service after this picture was taken at Doncaster Shed on 24th March 1963. The A.W.S. receiver and guard plate can clearly be seen beneath the front coupling. This equipment had finally been fitted to all the A4s by 1960.

Gavin Morrison

60016
SILVER KING

Plate 100 (Right): As soon as the first four A4s were in service, No. 2511 *Silver King* was sent to Gateshead, the other three remaining at King's Cross. *Silver King* was on standby in case one of the three King's Cross A4s failed on the 'Silver Jubilee'. After the 10.00 departure of the 'up' 'Silver Jubilee', *Silver King* often worked a 'down' Edinburgh express, returning with a late afternoon train from Edinburgh, which it took as far as Leeds. It is seen on this duty near Low Fell, in 1936, in its original livery.

W. B. Greenfield, NELPG Collection

Plate 101 (Below): A fine action picture of No. 2511, bursting out of the tunnel at Hadley Wood in 1939, heading the 'down' 'Flying Scotsman'. It had been repainted in Garter blue in August 1938 and it carried this livery until April 1943, when it was given war-time black livery.

C. R. L. Coles

Plate 102 (Left): Silver King was allocated in the North East, mainly at Gateshead, until October 1963, when it was transferred to Scotland. On 25th September 1960, it is seen in very shabby external condition, leaving Lincoln with a King's Cross – Newcastle train which had been diverted because of engineering works on the East Coast main line.

T. Boustead

Plate 103 (Right): On 2nd August 1961, it is seen standing outside its home depot of Gateshead with the 'cods-mouth' open for servicing purposes. Of the first four A4s, it was the only one ever to run without a corridor tender, when in June 1948 its corridor tender was exchanged for a streamlined non-corridor tender.

Gavin Morrison

Plate 104 (Below): On 22nd July 1963, shortly before being transferred to Scotland, Silver King is seen just after arrival at Edinburgh Waverley heading the 07.52 from Newcastle Tyne Commission Quay.

John Whiteley

60017
SILVER FOX

Plate 105 (Left): In 1936, No. 2512 *Silver Fox* is seen near Barnby Moor heading the 'Silver Jubilee'. Only the first four 'silver' A4s and also Nos. 4491-7 were given new corridor tenders, the corridor tenders fitted to the remaining A4s having previously been attached to non-streamlined Pacifics.

A. G. Ellis Collection

Plate 106 (Above): Again seen on 'Silver Jubilee' duties, this time on 14th July 1937, approaching Finsbury Park with the 'down' train.

J. P. Wilson

Plate 107 (Left): For just over twelve months, from September 1950, No. 60017 ran in BR blue livery, but in this picture taken on 2nd May 1953, it is in the standard BR green livery. It is climbing past Little Ponton towards Stoke Tunnel heading the 'up' 'Flying Scotsman'.

J. P. Wilson

Plate 108 (Above): On 18th June 1955, *Silver Fox* makes a vigorous departure from Grantham, heading an 'up' Leeds express. When it was brand new this locomotive was fitted with two stainless steel replicas of a fox, one on each side of the boiler casing, clearly seen in this picture. These had been supplied by Samuel Fox and Co. Limited, Steel Manufacturers.

T. G. Hepburn, Rail Archive Stephenson

Plate 109 (Left): After experiments with the smokebox arrangements on several A4s during the 1950s, in an attempt to improve the steaming qualities, it was finally decided in 1957 to fit all the single chimney A4s with Kylchap double blastpipes and chimneys, and No. 60017 was the first to be dealt with, in May 1957. In this picture it is passing Wortley South heading the 'up' 'White Rose' on 5th October 1962. *Silver Fox* was allocated to King's Cross from new until June 1963, when in common with the other surviving King's Cross A4s it was transferred to New England. It had the distinction of being the last A4 to depart from King's Cross on a normal service train, on 29th October 1963, when it headed the 18.40 to Leeds. Shortly afterwards it was withdrawn, and as with the other three 'silver' King's Cross A4s, it was cut up at Doncaster. The other 'silver' A4, No. 60016, was cut up by a scrap merchant in Scotland.

Gavin Morrison

60018 SPARROW HAWK

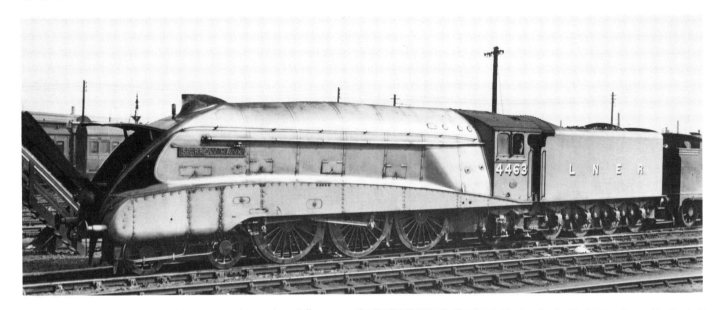

Plate 110 (Above): Seen at Heaton not long after delivery, in its original Garter blue livery, *Sparrow Hawk* was probably the least photographed of all the A4s. Throughout its entire life it was continually transferred between Gateshead and Heaton and rarely hit the limelight.

W. B. Greenfield, NEPLG Collection

Plate 111 (Right): Not in war-time black livery, as might first appear, No. 60018 is in BR green, but in filthy external condition, so typical of Gateshead at this period. It is seen on 16th August 1960, near Northallerton, returning to Tyneside, with an express from King's Cross. Its final transfer to Gateshead had taken place in November 1945, from where it was withdrawn in June 1963.

R. H. Leslie

Plate 112 (Below): A somewhat forlorn sight at Doncaster on 7th July 1963, it is awaiting its fate at the hand of the cutters torch. By todays standards, how strange it is to see such a locomotive awaiting scrap, complete with all its plates, no doubt now cherished by enthusiasts.

Gavin Morrison

60019 BITTERN

Plate 113 (Right): No. 4464 *Bittern* was delivered at the end of 1937, and by the summer of 1938, when all thirty-five A4s were in service, it was the only member of the class to be allocated to Heaton. It was often used on the 08.15 from Newcastle to King's Cross on alternate weekdays, returning the following day with the 'down' 'Flying Scotsman'. On 4th July 1938, it is seen near Low Fell, in its original blue livery, heading what is believed to be the 08.15 from Newcastle.

W. B. Greenfield, NELPG Collection

Plate 114 (Above): *Bittern* was allocated to Heaton until being moved to Gateshead in March 1943, where it remained until being transferred to Scotland in October 1963. On 21st July 1963, under a very light mid-summer sky, it is preparing to leave Edinburgh Waverley with the 23.13 to Carstairs, where the train joined the 23.40 from Glasgow to Manchester and Liverpool.

John Whiteley

Plate 115 (Right): In November 1963, it had been transferred to Aberdeen Ferryhill for use on the three hour services to Glasgow. Beautifully turned out, it is seen on 30th May 1966, nearing Gleneagles, heading the 'up' 'Granite City'.

John Whiteley

Plate 116 (Above): Another picture of No. 60019 on a three hour express from Aberdeen to Glasgow, this time the 'up' 'Bon Accord'. It is seen accelerating away from its stop at Stirling, on 20th April 1965.

John Whiteley

Plate 117 (Left): No. 60019 was one of the last two A4s which were officially withdrawn in September 1966, the other being No. 60024. Shortly after withdrawal, it was purchased by a private owner, and hauled several enthusiasts specials, until a ban on preserved steam movements was imposed by BR towards the end of 1967. In this photograph, taken on 16th July 1967, it is approaching Beattock on the West Coast main line with an RCTS special from Leeds to Scotland.

John Whiteley

Plate 118 (Right): After working its last train between Glasgow and Aberdeen, *Bittern* came south to York where arrangements had been made for its new owner, Mr G. S. Drury, to keep it in one of the roundhouses. Surprisingly, however, on 5th September 1966, it was used on an afternoon York – Healey Mills freight in place of the booked V2, and it is seen in this picture arriving at Healey Mills.

J. R. Livesey

60020 GUILLEMOT

Plate 119 (Left): No. 4465 was one of the last batch of fourteen A4s (Nos 4462-9, 4499, 4500 and 4900-3) all of which were given Garter blue livery with dark red wheels, and the numbers and letters in gold transfers with red shading. It is seen in this condition on 10th August 1938, with a full head of steam, awaiting to depart from Grantham with an 'up' express.

T. G. Hepburn,
Rail Archive Stephenson

Plate 120(Right): Guillemot spent all its working life allocated to the North East, mainly at Gateshead, but with just a short spell towards the end of the war at Heaton. In this picture, taken on 14th May 1960, it is heading a 'down' express, passing Muskham Troughs, north of Newark.

T. Boustead

Plate 121 (Below): By 1957 it had been fitted with a double chimney, and is seen here in June 1959, heading a King's Cross – Newcastle express, having just passed Potters Bar.

D. Cross

Plate 122 (Right): The 'up' 'Heart of Midlothian', formed of twelve all maroon coaches is hurried south, past Tollerton, towards York, on 6th August 1961, by No. 60020.

Gavin Morrison

Plate 123 (Below): No. 60020 is seen returning to Tyneside on 24th June 1961, at the head of the 'down' 'Flying Scotsman' passing Welwyn Garden City. This A4 was one of five, Nos. 3, 12, 14, 20, 31, which had the dimension of the middle cylinder lined up from 18½ in. to-17in. in 1947. Both *Guillemot* and *Commonwealth of Australia* retained these lined up middle cylinders for the rest of their lives, but the other three reverted to normal after a few years.

R. H. Leslie

Plate 124 (Right): On shed at Doncaster on 24th March 1963. *Guillemot* was one of the last fourteen A4s, all of which were initially attached to streamlined non-corridor tenders which had a coal capacity of nine tons. This locomotive retained its non-corridor tender for its entire working life. The tender to which it was coupled was a new one, built specifically for an A4, with the hand rails 4ft. 6in. long, matching the handrails on the cab. The handrails on the second-hand tenders, which had originally been fitted to A1s and A3s were slightly shorter at 4ft. 3in.

Gavin Morrison

60021
WILD SWAN

Plate 125 (Left): Only a few weeks after entering service, No. 4467 is seen awaiting departure from Newcastle Central on 19th March 1938, heading a southbound express. The lower part of the opening casing at the front does not appear to have been correctly closed and secured. In this picture the long pair of guardirons at the front end, to which the outside cylinder drain pipes were clipped, can be seen. In later years, these guardirons were removed and the outside cylinder drainpipes were consequently shortened and clipped together.

W. B. Greenfield, NEPLG Collection

Plate 126 (Below): On 7th May 1949, No. 60021 *Wild Swan* is climbing past Saltersford, shortly after leaving Grantham with an 'up' Newcastle train. By this time it has been repainted in blue livery following war-time black, and the lettering 'British Railways' can just be seen on the tender.

J. P. Wilson

Plate 127 (Right): In May 1963, *Wild Swan* is ready to depart from King's Cross with the 18.26 to Doncaster.

C. R. L. Coles

Plate 128 (Below): Resplendent in BR green with the early emblem on the tender, and still with single chimney, it is seen climbing Holloway Bank in fine style with an afternoon express to Leeds.

D. M. C. Hepburne-Scott,
Rail Archive Stephenson

Plate 129 (Above): A fine view of the north end of Peterborough sees No. 60021 approaching with the 'up' 'Norseman' on 16th August 1958.
P. H. Groom

Plate 130 (Left): The 12.30 to King's Cross is seen leaving Leeds Central behind No. 60021 in March 1961. When King's Cross shed closed in June 1963, No. 60021 was transferred to New England, but only survived for another few months.
Gavin Morrison

60022 MALLARD

Plate 131 (Left): Bearing in mind the A4s appeared shortly after Gresley's P2s, it is somewhat surprising that the Kylchap arrangement of double blastpipe and chimney was not fitted to the A4s when they first appeared. However, early in 1938 drawings were prepared for this arrangement to be fitted to No. 4468 *Mallard* which was then being constructed. In this picture, taken on 18th September 1938, it is inside the paint shop at Doncaster.

W. B. Greenfield,
NELPG Collection

Plate 132 (Right): After delivery, No. 4468 was allocated to Doncaster, running in their top link with a regular driver, J. Duddington. In June 1938, it was selected by Gresley for braking tests between London and Peterborough culminating in a premeditated fast run down the bank from Stoke Tunnel, having turned and prepared for this run at Barkston. The outcome of this run on 3rd July 1938, is now legendary. Suffice it to say that *Mallard* claimed the world speed record for steam traction which stands to this day, a maximum of 126m.p.h. having been attained. Here it is seen on 15th May 1939, at Nottingham Victoria with a Leicester – Sheffield slow, after having been on exhibition at Leicester.

J. P. Wilson

Plate 133 (Right): Plaques commemorating the run of 3rd July 1938, were fitted to the sides of the boiler casings in 1948. Seen here on 7th May 1949, as No. E22, it is approaching Grantham at the head of the 'down' 'Queen of Scots Pullman'.

J. P. Wilson

Plate 134 (Left): No. E22 is seen at Doncaster shed on 3rd July 1948. Under the first 1946 renumbering scheme all the A4s were to be numbered 580-613 in order of building, but as can be seen from the summary on Page 4, only four actually carried these numbers, and then only for a very short time. The second 1946 renumbering scheme commenced in May 1946 and was completed in January 1947. Nos. 1 – 7 were allocated to A4s which had already been named after high-ranking Company Officials, No. was chosen for *Dwight D. Eisenhower*, Nos. 9 – 1 were for the five engines which had been selected in 1937 for use on the 'Coronation', and the remainder Nos. 14 – 34 were allocated to the remaining A4s in ascending order of their original running numbers. After Nationalisation, 60,000 was added to the numbers, but as an interim measure, immediately after Nationalisation four A4s were given the prefix 'E' above their number. The other locomotives so treated were E4, E21 and E27.

J. P. Wilson

Plate 135 (Right): Having been allocated initially to Doncaster, and then to Grantham, *Mallard* was transferred to King's Cross in April 1948, having been coupled to a corridor tender the previous month. On 12th March 1959, it is seen shortly after leaving Cambridge with a 'slow' for King's Cross.

D. M. C. Hepburne-Scott,
Rail Archive Stephenson

Plate 136 (Below): At the head of a King's Cross – Newcastle express, it is seen rushing past Potters Bar in July 1960.

D. Cross

Plate 137 (Left): On 3rd March 1963, *Mallard* is seen between duties at Doncaster shed. In the two pictures on this page it can be seen that No. 60022 has now been coupled to a non-corridor tender, the one which was coupled to No. 60003 when it was withdrawn in December 1962. This particular tender was built new in 1938 and was originally coupled to No. 4467, as seen in *Plate 125.*

Gavin Morrison

Plate 138 (Below): On 2nd June 1962, it is departing from King's Cross with a special to Aberdeen which it was scheduled to haul non-stop as far as Edinburgh. After it was withdrawn for preservation in April 1963, it was restored at Doncaster to its original external appearance for static exhibition, firstly at Clapham, and now at the National Railway Museum in York. At the time of writing there appears to be a distinct possibilty that *Mallard* will be restored to full working order to enable a run to be made on the East Coast main line to commemorate the 50th Anniversary of attaining its world speed record for steam traction.

B. Stephenson

60023 GOLDEN EAGLE

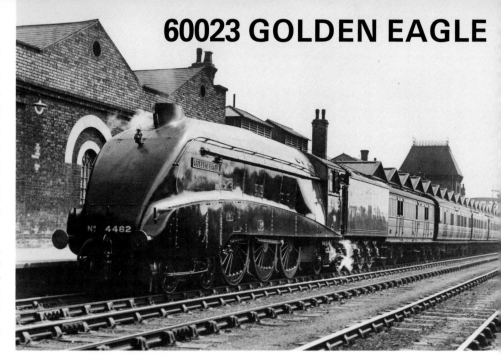

Plate 139 (Right): Following the introduction of the first four 'silver' A4s during 1935, No. 4482 was the first of a further batch of 17 A4s which were ordered during 1936 and entered traffic as Nos. 4482 – 98. These engines were intended for use on ordinary passenger duties which would comprise trains of varnished teak coaching stock. Clearly, therefore, silver grey livery would be far from an ideal match, and it was, therefore, decided to paint them in standard LNER passenger green livery with black and white lining and gold figures and letters with red shading. In the event, however, only the first six of this batch, Nos. 4482 – 87, followed by a further three, Nos. 4493 – 95, appeared in this green livery because Nos. 4488 – 92 were then selected for use on the 'Coronation', and painted Garter blue as previously described. No. 4482 is seen in this green livery at Peterborough North heading a 'down' slow on 18th August 1937.
T. G. Hepburn, Rail Archive Stephenson

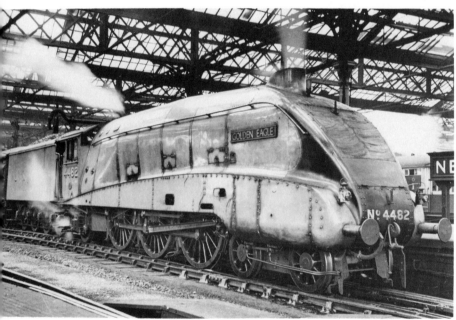

Plate 140 (Left): After the decision to standardise wit Garter blue livery for all the A4s, No. 4482 was repainted i January 1938. On 6th August 1938, it is standing insid Newcastle Central at the end of an express for Edinburgh.
W. B. Greenfield, NELPG Collectio

Plate 141 (Right): Now with double chimney and in BR livery it is passing Croft Spa on 30th July 1960, heading an Edinburgh – King's Cross express.
R. H. Leslie

Plate 142 (Right): Glinting in the late afternoon sun on 26th June 1954, No. 60023 arrives at Grantham with an 'up' express.

P. H. Wells

Plate 143 (Below): On 28th March 1959, *Golden Eagle* approaches its Retford stop with a King's Cross – Glasgow train, the driver having opened the regulator briefly after being checked by the signal in the distance.

T. Boustead

Plate 144 (Right): Well off the beaten track for an A4, No. 60023 is seen at Skipton on Sunday, 30th June 1963, heading the 'Three Summits Tour', a special organised by the R.C.T.S. *Golden Eagle* hauled the train on the outward journey from Leeds to Carlisle, and covered the 48.3 miles from Ais Gill Summit to Carlisle in the astonishing time of 42 minutes 12 seconds, with only one injector working and having suffered a signal check costing about 1¼ minutes on the approach to Carlisle Station. In fact, the 40.9 miles from Mallerstang Box to Cumwhinton was covered in 31 minutes 17 seconds, an average speed of 78.4m.p.h. which is generally thought to be the line record for this section. In October 1963, No. 60023 was transferred to Scotland from Gateshead, where it had been since 1942. Initially it was put in store at Bathgate, but by the summer of 1964, was back in traffic having been allocated to Aberdeen. It only saw one summer of services between Aberdeen and Glasgow, and was withdrawn in October 1964.

Gavin Morrison

60024
KINGFISHER

Plate 145 (Left): No. 4483 Kingfisher spent about one year in green livery, but in January 1938 it was repainted Garter blue, as seen in this picture of it leaving Newcastle in June 1938 with the 'down' 'Flying Scotsman'. The external beading along the edge of the corridor tender, built late in 1928, for use with non-streamlined Pacifics, can clearly be seen in this picture.
W. B. Greenfield, NELPG Collection

Plate 146 (Right): Kingfisher spent most of its time in Scotland, although it had brief spells at both King's Cross and Doncaster just before the war. In this picture taken on 3rd September 1957, it is passing through Princess Street Gardens, having just left Edinburgh Waverley with the 16.15 express to Aberdeen. In October 1954, plaques of the badge of H.M.S. Kingfisher were fitted on each side of the boiler casing, as can be seen in this picture.

P. H. Groom

Plate 147 (Left): 1960 was intended to be the last summer of steam haulage on the 'Elizabethan'. However, as the 1961 summer services approached, not all the replacement diesels were ready, with the result that 1961 turned out to be the last summer of A4s working this train. This picture was taken on 18th July 1961, and sees Kingfisher awaiting departure from Edinburgh Waverley on its scheduled non-stop run to King's Cross. Departure time from Edinburgh was 09.30, and 6½ hours was allowed for the journey of 392.7 miles.

John Whiteley

Plate 148 (Right): On 17th July 1961, the day before the previous picture was taken, No. 60024 is working the north-bound 'Elizabethan' and is seen climbing Holloway Bank shortly after leaving King's Cross. Its tender has been particularly well coaled for its long non-stop journey to Edinburgh.

P. H. Groom

Plate 149 (Above): On 26th March 1966, No. 60024 worked an A4 Preservation Society Rail Tour and is seen climbing from Weymouth. The ten coach train of all green Southern stock is being banked by BR Standard Class 5 No. 73114.

B. Stephenson

Plate 150 (Right): No. 60024 finished its days working from Aberdeen Ferryhill, mainly on the 3 hour expresses to Glasgow Buchanan Street. On 27th May 1966, it is leaving Gleneagles with the 'up' 'Grampian', and at the beginning of September 1966 was one of the only two surviving A4s, the other being No. 60019. Later in September of that year they were both withdrawn.

John Whiteley

60025 FALCON

Plate 151 (Above): No. 4484 *Falcon* ran in its original green livery until being repainted Garter blue in December 1937. Here it is passing Low Fell crossing heading a nine coach formation of the 'up' 'Coronation' on 21st July 1939.

W. B. Greenfield, NELPG Collection

Plate 152 (Below): *Falcon* was coupled to a corridor tender for its entire working life, and in this 1952 picture it is passing a lovely example of a G.N. somersault signal as it approaches Brookmans Park with the 'down' 'Tees-Tyne Pullman'.

F. R. Hebron, Rail Archive Stephenson

Plate 153 (Above): Again seen on prestige Pullman duty, it is leaving King's Cross with a good head of steam in August 1953 heading the 'down' 'Yorkshire Pullman'.

C. R. L. Coles

Plate 154 (Below): No doubt much to the delight of the local train spotting fraternity seen on the platform, No. 60025 is entering Lincoln on 1st July 1957, with the 'up' 'Flying Scotsman' which had been diverted due to engineering repairs on Newark Dyke Bridge.

J. P. Wilson

Plate 155 (Top): A4s were not often seen on humble freight duties, but in June 1959 No. 60025 is caught by the camera at Greenwood heading an 'up' loose-coupled freight.

D. Cross

Plate 156 (Centre): Beautifully turned out by King's Cross, in a condition appropriate for use on the 'Flying Scotsman', *Falcon* is climbing Holloway Bank on 16th September 1960, having just emerged from Copenhagen Tunnel.

D. M. C. Hepburne-Scott, Rail Archive Stephenson

Plate 157 (Right): Again seen in commendably clean external condition, typical of King's Cross top shed at the period, No. 60025 is leaving Leeds Central on 24th April 1961, with the 12.30 to King's Cross. *Falcon* was allocated to King's Cross from May 1950 until June 1963 when it was transferred to New England shortly before withdrawal late in 1963.

Gavin Morrison

60026 MILES BEEVOR

Plate 158 (Left): As originally turned out in lined green livery, No. 4485 *Kestrel* is taking water inside Newcastle Central whilst heading a 'down' passenger train. This view shows its corridor tender with the circular window in the upper right-hand corner clearly visible. This was one of the corridor tenders which was built in 1928 for a non-streamlined Pacific. Before any of these 1928 tenders were coupled to the A4s, they were modified with additional streamlined plating at the top, both at the front and the rear, to correspond with the design of the new streamlined corridor tenders.

W. B. Greenfield, NELPG Collection

Plate 159 (Right): Having been repainted Garter blue in December 1937, No. 4485 is seen leaving King's Cross in June 1938 with the 'down' 'Coronation', under the watchful eye of several interested onlookers.

W. B. Greenfield, NELPG Collection

Plate 160 (Left): *Kestrel* was renamed *Miles Beevor* in November 1947, after a high ranking official of the LNER, and on 8th March 1950, it is seen leaving Grantham with the 'up' 'Northumbrian'. When it was renamed, it was repainted in Garter blue livery, but in September 1949, was again repainted, this time in a slightly darker BR blue livery with the standard black and white lining. It was finally repainted dark green in January 1953 after it had been decided that the blue livery did not wear particularly well in service.

J. P. Wilson

Plate 161 (Left): Just after being coupled to a stream-lined non-corridor tender, but still in BR blue livery, No. 60026 is approaching Grantham on 4th October 1952, with a 'down' relief to the 'Northumbrian'.

J. P. Wilson

Plate 162 (Above): A fine picture taken on 23rd May 1962, sees No. 60026 in sparkling BR green livery on a rake of all maroon coaches. It is climbing past Belle Isle having just emerged from Gasworks Tunnel with a 'down' express.

D. M. C. Hepburne-Scott, Rail Archive Stephenson

Plate 163 (Left): *Miles Beevor* was another King's Cross A4 which ended up at Aberdeen, and on 4th June 1965, it has just passed Hilton Junction, shortly after leaving Perth with the 'up' West Coast Postal.

John Whiteley

60027 MERLIN

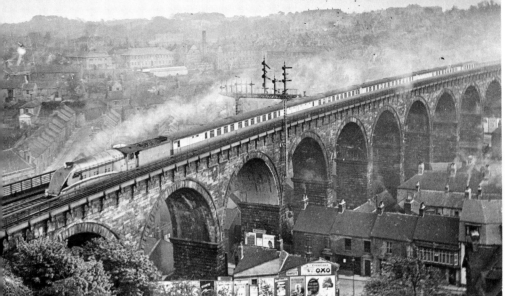

Plate 164 (Left): The 'Coronation' was the second LNER streamlined high speed train. It went into service on 3rd July 1937, between King's Cross and Edinburgh, leaving King's Cross at 16.00 and Edinburgh at 16.30. The nine coach train, including the streamlined observation car, was turned out in an attractive two-tone blue livery, the lower part in Garter blue, and the upper part Marlborough blue. This working was a considerably tougher proposition for both locomotive and crew than the lightweight 'Silver Jubilee' which only ran between King's Cross and Newcastle. In this May 1938 picture, No. 4486 Merlin is seen crossing Durham Viaduct, with the 'down' 'Coronation'.

W.B. Greenfield, NELPG Collection

Plate 165 (Above): Merlin was always allocated to Scottish sheds, initially Haymarket, and then finally St. Rollox and St. Margaret's for the last few years of its life. Whilst at Haymarket it was a regular performer on the non-stop services, 7th July 1952 was no exception, as it is seen leaving King's Cross with the 'down' 'Capitals Limited'. In May 1946, a plaque of the badge of H.M.S. Merlin, was fitted to each side of the cab, and subsequently moved to each side of the boiler casing, as seen here.

J.P. Wilson

Plate 166 (Right): In 1958, it is again seen on a non-stop working, this time the 'up' 'Elizabethan', passing Great Ponton.

T.G. Hepburn, Rail Archive Stephenson

Plate 167 (Left): The first of three pictures on this page, all showing *Merlin* on 'Elizabethan' services. Here it is seen passing through Doncaster on the 'up' train on 19th July 1958. For a few months in 1948, *Merlin* was coupled to a streamlined non-corridor tender, but for the remainder of its life it was coupled to a corridor tender, enabling use on these non-stop workings.

T.G. Hepburn, Rail Archive Stephenson

Plate 168 (Below): In September 1958, it is near Brookmans Park, again on the 'up' 'Elizabethan'.

D. Cross

Plate 169 (Left): On 23rd August 1968, some permanent-way men are taking a breather at Grantshouse as No. 60027 *Merlin* rushes past with the 'up' 'Elizabethan'. It clearly has plenty of coal in its tender but still has a long way to go to King's Cross. No. 60027 and No. 60031 were subjected to the final detail livery change during their last few months in service. A yellow diagonal stripe was painted across the cab sides denoting that they were prohibited from working south of Crewe beneath the overhead electrification, hardly a section of line normally associated with A4s!

R. H. Leslie

60028 WALTER K. WHIGHAM

Plate 170 (Left): No. 4487 *Sea Eagle* is approaching Manors soon after leaving Newcastle Central, on 10th September 1938, heading the 'down' 'Flying Scotsman'. It entered service in green livery but was re-painted Garter blue in February 1938.

W. B. Greenfield, NELPG Collection

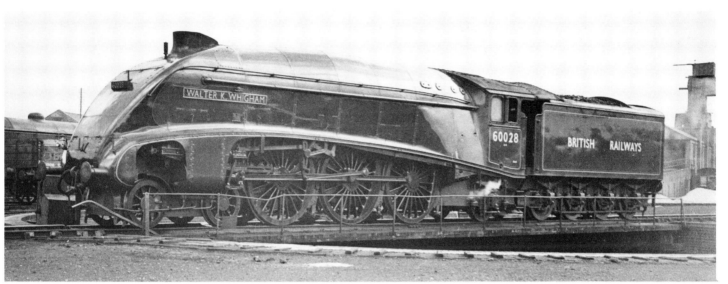

Plate 171 (Above): In October 1947, the name *Sea Eagle* was changed to *Walter K. Whigham*, another high ranking official of the LNER. Shortly after Nationalisation, it was one of four A4s, Nos. 60024/7/8/9 which were painted in an experimental purple livery. The lining out on the cab and tender was red, cream and grey. The running-board was lined out similarly and taken in front of the cylinders. 'British Railways' was lettered on the side of the tender, and on 17th June 1948, No. 60028 is seen in this condition standing on the turntable at Grantham.

J. P. Wilson

Plate 172 (Right): On 7th April 1950, it accelerates away from Grantham with a 'down' express, still painted in purple livery. All four A4s which had been painted in purple livery were repainted in BR blue between January 1950 and October 1950.

P. H. Wells

Plate 173 (Left): In September 1959, no[w] having been fitted with a double chimney, N[o] 60028 is hurrying the afternoon King's Cross–Niddre goods through Hadley Wood station. Th[is] express goods was diagrammed for a Pacifi[c,] often an A4.

D. Cros[s]

Plate 174 (Right): On 17th July 1961, the last summer of steam on the 'Elizabethan', it is seen, positively gleaming, inside Edinburgh Waverley, awaiting departure with the 'up' train.

John Whiteley

Plate 175 (Below): No. 60028 races past Abbots Ripton with the 'up' 'Elizabethan' on 21st June 1961. It had been allocated to King's Cross from May 1948, and ended its days there when it was withdrawn in December 1962.

R. H. Leslie

60029 WOODCOCK

Plate 176 (Left): On 2nd April 1938, No. 4493 *Woodcock* is preparing to leave Newcastle Central with an 'up' express. It is seen in its original green livery which was replaced by Garter blue, in July 1938.

W. B. Greenfield, NELPG Collection

Plate 177 (Below): A fine picture of No. 60029 taken in 1949, the year after Nationalisation. It is passing Hadley Wood with the 'down' 'Yorkshire Pullman'. In this picture it is painted in the short-lived purple livery, as described in *Plate 171*. As luck would have it, all four A4s which were given purple livery in 1948, were originally turned out in LNER green, and all these four were given no fewer than six different liveries throughout their lives. The only livery which was never applied to these A4s was grey, which was of course only given to the first four A4s when they originally entered service.

F. R. Hebron, Rail Archive Stephenson

Plate 178 (Left): Still in purpl livery, *Woodcock* is seen passin High Dyke shortly before plungin into Stoke Tunnel, heading the 'up 'Flying Şcotsman' on 4th Augu: 1948. It is hard to believe that onl twenty years after this photograp was taken, working steam wa eliminated from BR.

T. G. Hepburn
Rail Archive Stephenso

Plate 179 (Above): The afternoon King's Cross - Niddre goods has just passed Potters Bar i September 1959, behind No. 60029 *Woodcock*.
D. Cros:

Plate 180 (Left): In this picture, No. 60029 is seen passing Holbeck High Level, shortly after leaving Leeds Central, heading the 'up' 'White Rose' on 20th April 1961.

Gavin Morrison

60030 GOLDEN FLEECE

Plate 181 (Left): When No. 4495 entered service in August 1937, it was named *Great Snipe* and painted in green livery. Soon after entering service, however, along with No. 4496, it was selected for use on the third and final LNER streamlined train, the 'West Riding Limited'. This was an eight coach train which ran between Bradford, Leeds and King's Cross, A4 hauled only between Leeds and King's Cross. As a result of being selected for use on this streamlined train, it was repainted Garter blue and renamed *Golden Fleece*. Here it is heading the 'down' 'Flying Scotsman' over Werrington Troughs on 4th July 1938.

T. G. Hepburn,
Rail Archive Stephenson

Plate 182 (Right): No. 4495 *Golden Fleece* is approaching Manors shortly after leaving Newcastle Central on 9th June 1939, heading a 'down' express. In the distance, just above the cab of No. 4495, another A4 can be seen crossing High Level Bridge, no doubt on its way either from or to Gateshead motive power depot.

W. B. Greenfield, NELPG Collection

Plate 183 (Below): In 1945, No. 4495 has just passed Potters Bar with a 'down' Leeds and Bradford express. It is painted in war-time black livery, which replaced Garter blue in December 1941, and which it carried until again being repainted Garter blue in December 1946. Note the initials 'N.E.' on the tender.

C. R. L. Coles

Plate 184 (Left): On 9th July 1938, in Garter blue livery, *Golden Fleece* has just emerged from Askham Tunnel heading a 'down' express.

T. G. Hepburn, Rail Archive Stephenson

Plate 185 (Below): This A4 was originally allocated to Doncaster, but after being selected for use on the 'West Riding Limited,' it was transferred to King's Cross. For the rest of its career it alternated between King's Cross and Grantham, until being withdrawn from King's Cross in December 1962. Here it is seen at Grantham motive power depot on 31st May 1953, having been repainted BR dark green and with the original lion and wheel emblem on the tender.

J. P. Wilson

Plate 186 (Below): Beautifully turned out by King's Cross, and with an extremely generous supply of coal in the tender, seemingly almost exceeding the loading gauge limits, No. 60030 is near Finsbury Park heading the 'down' 'Tees-Tyne Pullman' on 30th May 1960.

P. H. Groom

Plate 187 (Top): On 8th August 1959, now fitted with a double chimney, it is climbing towards Stoke Tunnel, near Little Ponton, with an 'up' express.

T. G. Hepburn, Rail Archive Stephenson

Plate 188 (Centre): Heading the 'up' 'Flying Scotsman' on 16th August 1960, No. 60030 is seen racing through Thirsk.

R. H. Leslie

Plate 189 (Right): *Golden Fleece* was withdrawn in December 1962, and on 3rd February 1963, complete with plates, is at Doncaster awaiting cutting up.

Gavin Morrison

60031 GOLDEN PLOVER

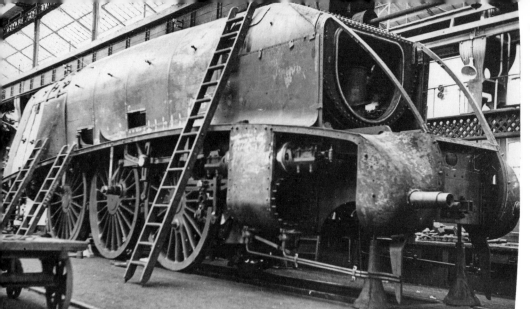

Plate 190 (Left): No. 4497 *Golden Plover* entered service in October 1937 in Garter blue livery and coupled to a corridor tender. In this picture, taken earlier in 1937, it is seen under construction at Doncaster. From this picture it can be seen how the streamlined casing at the front projected beyond the front of the smokebox.
W. B. Greenfield, NELPG Collection

Plate 191 (Right): When delivered, *Golden Plover* was allocated to Haymarket where it remained until February 1962, when it was transferred to St. Rollox. It was always coupled to a corridor tender and was a regular performer on the non-stop services between Edinburgh and King's Cross. Early in its career, it incredibly worked thirty-nine consecutive round trips on the 'Coronation'. Here it is passing Essendine on 3rd September 1955, with an 'up' express.
P. H. Wells

Plate 192 (Below): Heading the 'down' 'Elizabethan' in July 1959, No. 60031 is passing Greenwood.
D. Cross

Plate 193 (Above):   Just after the start of its scheduled non-stop journey to Edinburgh, *Golden Plover* is passing Belle Isle on 29th June 1961, with the 'down' 'Elizabethan'.   *D. M. C. Hepburne-Scott, Rail Archive Stephenson*

Plate 194 (Below):   After it was transferred to St. Rollox it was often used on services between Dundee and Glasgow Buchanan Street, and on 21st August 1964, it is seen accelerating the 14.00 Dundee – Glasgow train away from its stop at Stirling.   *John Whiteley*

60032 GANNET

Plate 195 (Left): On 23rd May 1938, shortly after delivery, No. 4900 *Gannet* is nearing Peascliffe Tunnel, just after leaving Grantham, heading a Grantham – Doncaster slow. After delivery it was allocated to Doncaster, and in this picture is seen 'running-in' on one of its first workings.
T. G. Hepburn, Rail Archive Stephenson

Plate 196 (Right): In its original Garter blue livery, it is again seen nearing Peascliffe Tunnel, heading a 'down' express. All thirty-five A4s were in service by July 1938, and at that time, eleven were allocated to King's Cross, ten to Haymarket, eight to Gateshead, three to Doncaster, two to Grantham, and one to Heaton.
T. G. Hepburn, Rail Archive Stephenson

Plate 197 (Left): On 13th May 1939, *Gannet* nears Potters Bar heading the 'down' 'Yorkshire Pullman'.
J. G. Dewing

Plate 198 (Right): When *Gannet* was delivered, it was coupled to a streamlined non-corridor tender, which it retained until October 1952. It then alternated between being fitted with a corridor and a non-corridor tender, but in September 1955, it was again coupled to a corridor tender, which it then retained until withdrawal. After being coupled to a corridor tender, it was allocated to King's Cross and was used on the non-stop workings to Edinburgh. In this picture, taken on 23rd August 1960, it is approaching Grantshouse with the 'down' 'Elizabethan'. It has just crossed one of the bridges which had to be rebuilt following disastrous floods, which caused the collapse of many bridges on this section of the East Coast main line during the summer of 1948.

R. H. Leslie

Plate 199 (Below): No. 60032 *Gannet* appears to be priming badly in this photograph taken on 21st July 1962, shortly after it has emerged from Stoke Tunnel with an 'up' express.

Gavin Morrison

Plate 200 (Below): *Gannet* at rest, seen at Copley Hill motive power depot on 19th August 1961.

Gavin Morrison

Plate 201 (Below): *Gannet* at work, seen leaving Grantham Station with a 'down' express.

T. Boustead

60033 SEAGULL

Plate 202 (Left): No. 4902 *Seagull* was one of the last three A4s to be built, Nos. 4901-3, all of which were fitted with a double blastpipe and chimney when they were built like No. 4468 *Mallard* had been earlier, in 1938. These Kylchap-fitted A4s were very free-steaming engines, but because of the outbreak of the Second World War, followed by the death of Sir Nigel Gresley in 1941, the remaining A4s were not similarly treated until BR days, which then gave them a new lease of life. In October 1938, No. 4902 *Seagull* is passing Low Fell with a 'down' passenger train.

W. B. Greenfield, NELPG Collection

Plate 203 (Below): Initially coupled to a streamlined non-corridor tender, this was exchanged for a corridor tender in April 1948, enabling non-stop running between London and Edinburgh. In this picture taken in 1949, No. 60033 is passing Welwyn South in blue livery heading the 'up' 'Capitals Limited'.

F. R. Hebron, Rail Archive Stephenson

Plate 204 (Right): During April, May and June 1948, immediately after Nationalisation, the famous locomotive interchange trials took place in order to compare deigns of the 'Big Four', pending new standard locomotive designs for the Nationalised BR system. It was decided that a double chimney A4 would represent the newly formed Eastern Region, and *Mallard* was duly chosen, much to the dismay of the running staff at King's Cross who felt that this was not their best A4 at the time. During preliminary trials on the Western Region, *Mallard* failed on 28th April, and No. 60033 *Seagull* was substituted. *Seagull* completed all the dynamometer car trials on the Western Region, and in this picture is seen near Iver heading the 08.30 Plymouth – Paddington express on 7th May 1948.

F. R. Hebron,
Rail Archive Stephenson

Plate 205 (Above): *Seagull* commenced preliminary trial running on the Southern Region before the dynamometer trials proper, but failed, and this time *Mallard* was substituted. During the trials, however, *Mallard* failed and *Seagull* came to the rescue again, completing the two dynamometer car trials on the Southern. In this picture, however, it is back on familiar territory on the Eastern Region, leaving Grantham with an 'up' Leeds express on 18th June 1955.

J. P. Wilson

Plate 206 (Right): On 19th July 1958, No. 60033 is just south of Grantham heading the 16.12 Grantham – Peterborough local train, which at this time was a regular working for a Pacific, often an A4.

P. H. Groom

60034 LORD FARINGDON

Plate 207 (Left): No. 4903 *Peregrine* was the last A4 to be built, entering service in July 1938 in Garter blue livery and coupled to a streamlined non-corridor tender. For the first few years it was allocated to Doncaster, and is seen here on 18th September 1938. When this A4 was given its BR number, it was renamed *Lord Faringdon*, a name carried by a Great Central Class B3 until its withdrawal immediately before Nationalisation. Lord Faringdon had been Chairman of the Great Central and became one of the original LNER Directors.

W. B. Greenfield, NELPG Collection

Plate 208 (Above): The Euston – Carlisle dynamometer car trials during the 1948 exchanges were conducted during May, and No. 60034 was the A4 which was selected. During the week preceding the trials, *Lord Faringdon* was used on the 'down' 'Royal Scot' to enable the driver to learn the road. This picture was taken on 17th May 1948, and shows No. 60034 picking up water on Bushey Troughs heading the 'down' 'Royal Scot'.

F. R. Hebron, Rail Archive Stephenson

Plate 209 (Left): *Lord Faringdon* was also used in the 1948 trials between King's Cross and Leeds which were conducted with a dynamometer car in April. In this picture, taken on 19th April 1948, it is leaving King's Cross with the 13.20 to Leeds, with the dynamometer car immediately behind the tender.

F. R. Hebron, Rail Archive Stephenson

Plate 210 (Right): No. 60034 was the last A4 to run in LNER Garter blue livery, with the lettering 'British Railways' on the tender, as seen in the previous picture. It appeared in BR blue in December 1950, and finally succumbed to standard BR dark green in August 1952. In this picture, taken on 20th May 1957, it is passing Little Bytham with a King's Cross – Edinburgh express.

P. H. Wells

Plate 211 (Left): On 6th August 1959, it is nearing Stoke Summit with a 'down' express. It has just passed Austerity 2-8-0 No. 90732 *Vulcan* heading a 'down' mixed freight.

T. Boustead

Plate 212 (Right): When King's Cross top shed closed in June 1963, No. 60034 was one of eleven A4s still in service there, which were transferred to New England. It was one of five remaining on the Eastern Region in October 1963, when it was transferred to Scotland. Initially it went to St. Margaret's, but in May 1964 it was transferred to Aberdeen Ferryhill where it was used on the 3 hour Glasgow expresses. Here it is seen leaving Stirling on 24th August 1964, heading the West Coast Postal.

John Whiteley

Plate 213 (Left): In the company of three Stanier Class 5s, it is seen on shed at Perth on 8th June 1965.

John Whiteley

Plate 214 (Left): No. 4469 *Gadwall* entered service in March 1938 in Garter blue livery, and was allocated to Gateshead. In the summer of 1938 it is seen passing Low Fell with an 'up' express.
W. B. Greenfield, NELPG Collection

Plate 215 (Right): Another 1938 picture sees No. 4469 *Gadwall* near Barnby Moor heading an 'up' express.
A. G. Ellis Collection

Plate 216 (Below): On 21st June 1939, No. 4469 *Sir Ralph Wedgwood* is leaving York with a southbound express. *Gadwall* was officially renamed *Sir Ralph Wedgwood* on 3rd March 1939, after the Chief General Manager of the LNER who had retired the previous day. It remained in Garter blue until April 1942, when it was repainted in war-time black. Sadly, this A4 did not survive the war, as it was damaged at York beyond economic repair during an air raid on 29th April 1942. It was, therefore, withdrawn from service and cut up, the name reappearing on No. 4466 in January 1944.

W. B. Greenfield, NELPG Collection